---  ✦  ---

"The fundamental thing is freedom!
In art there are millions of paths—as many
paths as there are artists."

—Rufino Tamayo

DIEGO ISAIAS HERNANDEZ MÉNDEZ, *Peligro de Corte Flores y Bajar Barriletes del Día de los Difuntos*
*(Danger in Picking Flowers and Bringing Down Kites on the Day of the Dead).*
2004. Oil on canvas. 20" x 26".
Collection of Charles Davey. www.artemaya.com.

# COME
# LOOK WITH ME

*Latin American Art*

Kimberly Lane

iᴥi Charlesbridge

*For my students, whose curiosity, insight,
and excitement when looking at art continually inspire me.*

—K. L.

Published by Charlesbridge
85 Main Street
Watertown, MA 02472
(617) 926-0329
www.charlesbridge.com

Library of Congress Cataloging-in-Publication Data

Lane, Kimberly.
   Come look with me : Latin American art / Kimberly Lane.
      p. cm.
   ISBN 978-1-890674-20-5 (reinforced for library use)
   1. Art, Latin American. 2. Art—Political aspects—Latin America. 3.
Art—Social aspects—Latin America. I. Title.
N6502.L36 2007
709.8—dc22                              2006034237

Printed in China
(hc) 10 9 8 7 6 5 4 3 2 1

Production & Design: Charles Davey *design* LLC

# Contents

# Preface

The history of art in Latin America stretches back thousands of years to such remarkable civilizations as the Olmec, Maya, Inca, and Aztec peoples. While COME LOOK WITH ME: *Latin American Art* focuses primarily on modern and contemporary Latin American art, the influence of this rich artistic tradition is apparent in the work of many of the artists represented here.

Rather than focus on one particular country's artistic tradition, this book provides an introduction to many of Latin America's greatest artists of the last two centuries. Some of the artists' names in this book may be familiar while others may not be found in traditional art history texts that focus on European and North American art.

The art in this book reflects some of the political, social, and cultural shifts in Latin America as it emerged from the colonial rule of the 16th, 17th, and 18th centuries and its countries developed national identities. Great political events such as the Mexican Revolution spurred changes in all aspects of life, including art. Some artists used their art to promote political and social changes; others explored different ways of representing the world.

Just as many Latin American countries have struggled with political, economic, and social change, so too have Latin American artists struggled to communicate their thoughts, experiences, and dreams. The artists in *Latin American Art* come from many different countries, cultures, and language areas. Some of them were self-taught; others studied with famous teachers around the world. Some never left their home countries, while others spent much of their lives traveling and living elsewhere.

The art also reflects a shift in thinking about the nature of art, when artists across Latin America, just as in Europe, began to challenge the notion that art had to reproduce reality. What the artists share, and what we can explore in this book, besides the many geographic locations, are the ways they have found to communicate these ideas.

# How to use this book

COME LOOK WITH ME: *Latin American Art* is part of a series of art appreciation books for children. This book presents an interactive way of looking at art. Each of the twelve artists is represented by a full-page color reproduction, which is accompanied by a brief biography and information about the artwork. The text may be read aloud by an adult or paraphrased to help guide children's conversations.

In addition to the background information, each image is accompanied by a set of questions intended to encourage thoughtful observation and stimulate conversation between adults and children. Like others in this series, this book may be shared with one child or a group of children. Encourage children to point to specific parts of an image while they discuss it. There are no right or wrong answers to the questions, and everyone will benefit from the different perspectives. To keep the interaction lively, it is best to limit each session to the discussion of two or three pieces of art.

The titles of the art reproduced in this book appear exactly as they are used by the institutions or individuals who own the original artworks. Some are translated into English from Spanish or Portuguese, others are not.

This book can be used at home, in the classroom, or in museums. Whenever possible, it is always ideal to see a work of art in person. The methods given here provide children a way of looking at original works of art and encourage them to share their understanding with others.

XUL SOLAR, *Drago*.
1927. Watercolor. 10" x 12⅝".
Fundación Pan Klub, Museo Xul Solar, Argentina.

What is happening in this scene?

What kind of creature do you see in this painting?

How many of the flags in this picture do you recognize?

Why are the sun and moon out at the same time?

Xul Solar (1887–1963) was born in Argentina. His father was German and his mother was Italian. When he was a boy, he invented a fantasy world to express his thoughts, visions, and feelings. He devoted his life to exploring and sharing his inner world with the hope that he could make the real world a better place. He expressed himself in poetry, architecture, music, painting, and his own invented languages. He even invented his own name! He was born Alejandro Schulz Solari, but as a young man he began calling himself "Xul Solar," which in the language he invented means "Light from the Other Side." He wanted to be like the sun, bringing light and energy to the world.

In 1912 Xul Solar left Argentina, and for twelve years he traveled in Europe studying art. He was influenced by many European artists, but he most admired the artist Paul Klee, who said that the artist's mission was to make the invisible visible. You can imagine how inspiring this was to Xul Solar, who had been trying to tell others about his own imaginary world in so many ways.

In *Drago* we see a mythical landscape. The sun and the moon share the same sky. In the title, Xul Solar uses one of his invented words to refer to the dragon that slithers across the sand surrounded by flags from North and South American and European countries. On its back stands a figure dressed in colorful garments, holding a tall staff. The rhythm of the dragon's body is echoed in the shape of the sky and the waves of the sea. The bright colors and geometric shapes in this watercolor painting are typical of Xul Solar's work.

After his return to Argentina in 1924, Xul Solar exhibited frequently in Buenos Aires, where he died in 1963. He became friends with the philosopher and writer Jorge Luis Borges, and the two remained close friends for the rest of their lives. Their art and writing had a strong influence on the visual art and literature of Argentina.

JOSÉ GUADALUPE POSADA, *Calavera Las Bicicletas*.
c. 1895. Ink on newsprint. 4" x 5".
Collection of Lisbeth and August Uribe, New York.

Who are these skeletons and what are they doing?

Does this picture seem funny or scary to you?

Why does one of the skeletons have wings and a long beard?

Why are some of the skeletons big and others small?

José Guadalupe Posada (1852–1913) was born in Aguascalientes in Central Mexico. When he was sixteen he was apprenticed to an artist who taught him how to make prints. Printmaking involves creating an image on a plate of wood, stone, or metal and then transferring that image to another surface, usually a piece of paper. Posada made his living by doing commercial work for many different kinds of clients. Soon his prints could be found on everything from advertisements for cigars to directions for magic tricks to recipes. His illustrations for song lyrics were particularly popular.

In addition to his commercial work, Posada liked to make prints that showed the lives of ordinary people of Mexico and ones that expressed his opinions about current events. He printed on brightly colored, inexpensive paper called broadsheets that he sold for as little as one cent. He wanted his prints to be affordable to everyone so that his message could reach many people. Posada often used satire in his work, meaning that he used humor to criticize the faults of people whom he felt deserved it.

Each year at the time of the festival of *Día de los Muertos* (Day of the Dead), when Mexican families remember their dead relatives, Posada would create new *calaveras* prints. A *calavera* is a skull or skeleton that is a symbol for the Day of the Dead holiday in Mexico and other parts of Latin America. Instead of creating sad or frightening images of death, Posada depicted funny *calavera* characters acting out many different human activities. People loved Posada's *calaveras* because he poked fun at everyone, even members of the government and other powerful people. In *Calavera Las Bicicletas*, Posada created *calaveras* designed to mock the popular newspapers of his time. Each newspaper has its own character, all pictured riding on bicycles, which Posada considered a dangerous craze.

Posada died penniless at age sixty-six. He left a legacy of thousands of prints that influenced many artists who came after him. He is revered to this day as one of Mexico's most important and beloved artists.

DIEGO RIVERA, *La Unión entre la Expresión Artistica del Norte y la Sur de este Continente* (*Marriage of the Artistic Expression of the North and of the South on this Continent*), detail.
1940. Al fresco on ten steel-framed panels. 1,800 square feet. City College of San Francisco. www.riveramural.com.

Is this a scene from real life?

Who do you think these people might be?

When do you think this scene might have taken place?

What activities are happening in this painting?

From the time he was nine years old, Diego Rivera (1886–1957) knew that he wanted to be an artist. While an art student, he studied the art of his own country, Mexico, before the Spanish invaded it in the 16th century. Rivera was fascinated with the "pre-Hispanic" art of the Olmec, Maya, and Aztec peoples, and collecting their art became a lifelong passion for him.

In 1907 Rivera traveled to Europe to study art. Three years later, there was a revolution in his homeland. Rivera wanted to make artwork that would celebrate the lives of ordinary people and inspire them to fight against injustice. He wanted his art to be seen by everyone, not just the few who could afford to buy paintings. In Italy Rivera had seen paintings done *al fresco*: that is, painted on the walls of buildings while the plaster was still wet. Rivera wanted to create huge murals in public places to communicate his ideas.

In 1921 he returned to Mexico, and the new president asked him and two other artists, David Alfaro Siqueiros and José Clemente Orozco, to create murals on public buildings. The three became known as *Los Tres Grandes*, and their work was called the Mexican mural movement.

This painting is a detail from a large mural that Rivera created in the United States in 1940. He called it *Marriage of the Artistic Expression of the North and of the South on this Continent*, and in it he showed scenes from North American history. This panel celebrates what many of the native peoples gave to their culture. Near the bottom Toltec artisans carve a large upright stone slab called a *stela*. Behind them a woman weaves on a loom. Near her others decorate a sculpture. Farther back Yaquis dancers and musicians perform a sacred deer dance, and a priest teaches to a ruling council. Great pyramids and cities stretch to mountains on the horizon.

Near the end of his life, Rivera built a museum to house his collection of the artwork of Mexico's native ancestors. Diego Rivera created paintings celebrating the lives, ideas, and works of the people of Mexico; his museum was his final gift to them.

AMELIA PELÁEZ, *Marpacífico (Hibiscus).*
1943. Oil on canvas. 45½" x 35".
Collection of the Art Museum of the Americas, Organization of American States.

What do you see in this painting?

What parts of a house can you find in this painting?

Where are the flowers in this painting?

How do the flowers stand out?

Amelia Peláez (1896–1968) was born on the east coast of the island of Cuba. Her father was a wealthy doctor, and the family had a comfortable life. When Amelia was nineteen, the family moved to a large house in a suburb outside Havana. Amelia's mother wanted all eleven of her children to pursue their own interests, so the family sent Amelia to school to study art. After graduating in 1924 she studied art first in New York, then in Europe.

In Europe, artists such as Pablo Picasso were experimenting with new, abstract ways of looking at things, and their art was called cubist. The traditional approach to painting a bowl of fruit would be to try to make the painting look as lifelike as possible from a single viewpoint. A cubist might show the table, bowl, and fruit from many different angles all together in one painting. Amelia's way of thinking about art was turned upside down. She was inspired by these new ideas and practiced using them in her own artwork.

After seven years away Amelia returned to Cuba. In most countries in the 1920s and 1930s, a woman was expected to stay at home and run her household. Amelia moved back into her family's home, where she lived with her mother and sisters. There she was freshly inspired to paint the Caribbean colors of Cuba. In her paintings she focused on the objects found all around her, such as flowers, fruit, gardens, and the architectural details of her house and of buildings in her neighborhood.

*Marpacífico (Hibiscus)* is an example of how Peláez combined subject matter from Cuba with the techniques and styles that she learned in Europe. The brilliant red of the hibiscus flowers shines out against the outlines of its petals like light coming through a stained glass window. Behind the plant we can make out the back, cushion, legs, and swirling lines of a wicker chair that seems all mixed up—seen from many angles at the same time. At the top we see a blue ceiling with the looping lines of fancy molding.

Amelia exhibited her work in Cuba and in the United States, and her artworks can be found today in major museums.

RUFINO TAMAYO, *Women of Tehuantepec.*
1939. Oil on canvas. 33⅞" x 57⅛".
Albright-Knox Art Gallery, Buffalo, New York. Room of Contemporary Art Fund, 1941.

Who are the people in this painting?

Why do two of the women have baskets on their heads?

Is this scene happening inside or outside?

Do these people know each other?

---

Rufino Tamayo (1899–1991) was born in the state of Oaxaca in southern Mexico. His family was descended from the Zapotecan Indians. When he was twelve his parents died, and he went to live with his aunt in Mexico City. There he attended school and worked for his aunt as a fruit vendor, but more than anything he loved to draw. As a young man Tamayo spent many hours in the National Archaeological Museum drawing objects from past Mexican civilizations such as the Olmec, Maya, and Aztec peoples. He loved the art of these native Mexican cultures so much that he was hired by the museum to draw many of the objects in their collection. The shapes, symbols, and ideas in the art of these pre-Hispanic civilizations had a huge impact on Tamayo's artwork throughout his life.

Although Tamayo is considered one of Mexico's greatest artists now, he was criticized when he was young. Well-known artists in the Mexican mural movement rejected him because his work used abstract shapes rather than realistic historical scenes. Tamayo believed that the most important thing about art is freedom. He said, "In art there are millions of paths—as many paths as there are artists." He left Mexico and traveled to Europe where he was inspired, as many Latin American artists were, by the modern art in Europe and by such artists as Picasso, Braque, and Cézanne, who did not feel that it was important to make paintings look "realistic."

In *Women of Tehuantepec* (tay-WAN-tay-peck), Tamayo combines modern European techniques with his passion for pre-Hispanic art. The people pictured here are from the area of Tehuantepec in southern Mexico. Tamayo did not try to make this painting look three-dimensional, but instead focused on showing the shapes and sunny colors of the fruits, flowers, and buildings.

In 1964 Tamayo returned to Mexico, where he lived for the rest of his life. The ideas about art had changed in Mexico, and he was celebrated and loved as a great artist in the later part of his life. In 1981 a museum was built in Mexico City to house his collection of his paintings.

TARSILA DO AMARAL, *Estrada de Ferro Central do Brasil (Central Railroad of Brazil).*
1924. Oil on canvas. 56" x 50".
Museu de Arte Contemporânea da Universidade de São Paulo, Brazil.

What kind of place do we see in this painting?

How would you describe the colors in this painting?

What can you find that is from nature? What objects are made by humans?

If you were in the painting, what sounds could you hear?

Tarsila do Amaral (1886–1973) was the daughter of a wealthy coffee rancher in São Paulo, Brazil. As a girl she often traveled to Europe. After finishing school in Spain, do Amaral returned to Brazil, but she was unsure what she wanted to do with her life. She took piano lessons, attended lectures, and copied pictures in her spare time. It was not until she began taking lessons with two local sculptors, when she was thirty years old, that do Amaral decided to be an artist.

Like many other artists of her time, do Amaral went to Europe to explore the most modern techniques and ideas in art. She made several trips between São Paolo and Paris, where she studied with artists such as Pablo Picasso and Fernand Léger. She began combining ideas from European styles such as cubism with the colors and subject matter of Brazil. She wanted to create a new, modern style so that Brazil could have "a type of painting that is truly our own."

In *Estrada de Ferro Central do Brasil (Central Railroad of Brazil)*, do Amaral combines mechanical objects such as telephone poles, a bridge, and train signals with things commonly found in the Brazilian landscape, such as coconut palms, houses, and churches. Notice how the strong black lines and bright red shapes make many of the mechanical objects stand out against the softer pinks, greens, and sandy browns in the countryside. Unlike a traditional landscape, in which the artist would try to show what the scene might look like if you were standing in it, do Amaral does not try to make this place look realistic. In her style, everything is simplified to its most basic shapes.

In addition to her painting, do Amaral worked as a rancher, illustrator, and newspaper columnist. She continued to make art throughout her life, and had a strong influence on Brazilian art. She died in São Paulo in 1973.

FRIDA KAHLO, *The Little Deer (La Venadita)*.
1946. Oil on canvas. 8¾" x 11¾".

What is happening in this scene?

How would you describe the creature in this painting?

Why do you think the artist put a human head on the body of a deer? Whose face could that be?

Who do you think shot the arrows?

Frida Kahlo (1907–1954) was born in a little town that at that time was on the outskirts of Mexico City. Though the name Frida means "peace" in German, her father's native language, Frida Kahlo's life was anything but peaceful. At the age of six, she contracted polio and was forced to stay in bed for nine months. Though she recovered, she never regained full strength in her right leg, which she hid by wearing long skirts and trousers.

When Kahlo was fifteen she began attending the National Preparatory School in Mexico City, the best school in all of Mexico. One day on her way home, her streetcar crashed. Kahlo almost died from her terrible injuries. After a month in the hospital, she went home, wearing a plaster cast over most of her body. Her mother gave her a special easel so she could paint lying down, and hung a mirror above her bed so she could use herself as a model. After three months she recovered and was able to paint standing up or sitting down, but she struggled with pain and health problems for the rest of her life.

*The Little Deer* was made in 1946, a year in which Kahlo's health was getting worse. Kahlo has painted her own face and head on the body of a deer. Though the deer's body has been pierced by many arrows, the animal is shown leaping through a forest. Kahlo portrays herself as a wounded creature, but one that is still very much alive. She sent the painting to friends with a note describing it as "a portrait of my sadness on the entire canvas."

Kahlo painted her own image in many paintings throughout her life. Some people thought her paintings seemed like dreams. Kahlo disagreed, saying, "I have never painted dreams. What I represented was my own reality."

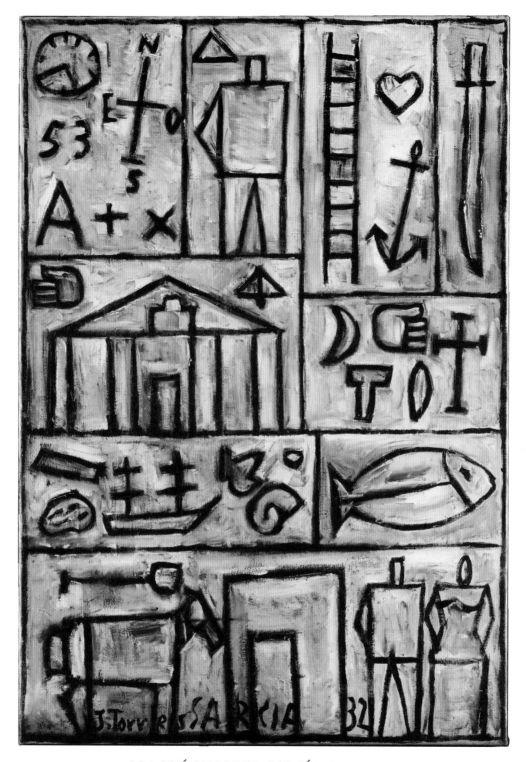

JOAQUÍN TORRES-GARCÍA, *Composition.*
1932. Oil on canvas. 28¼" x 19¾".
Digital Image © The Museum of Modern Art/Licensed by SCALA/Art Resource, NY.

What objects can you identify?

What do some of the symbols in this painting remind you of?

What cultures do you know of that use pictures or symbols in their writing or art?

Joaquín Torres-García (1874–1949) was born in Montevideo, Uruguay. His mother was from Uruguay and his father was from Catalan, in Spain. Torres-García moved to Barcelona, Spain, with his family when he was seventeen. He did not return to Uruguay for forty-three years. During that time he lived in six different countries on three different continents. He designed toys, worked as a teacher, made stained glass, and illustrated books.

Torres-García felt that what was most important about art was to communicate a message that was timeless and universal. He was deeply inspired by art from native Latin American cultures, such as the Olmec, Maya, and Inca, and thought that the symbols they used in their art could communicate better than words. For example, in a modern traffic signal, the picture of a person walking shows that it is safe to walk, no matter what language someone speaks. Torres-García used simple symbols to communicate messages that he thought would make sense to anyone from anywhere.

*Composition* is an example of Torres-García's ideas in action. Horizontal and vertical lines divide the painting into rectangular sections. Each section contains one or more line drawings that represent objects such as a clock, a ladder, or a person. These pictures are called ideograms, because each one represents an idea. Torres-García is not trying to show us what a ship looks like, but instead is using the ideogram of a ship to make us think about ideas such as exploration and discovery. The clock might make us think about the passage of time.

In 1943 Torres-García founded an art studio called El Taller Torres-García where artists could collaborate with writers, musicians, and performers and work on sculpture, architecture, and painting. In the same year he published a book, *Universalismo Constructivo* (*The Constructive Universalism*), that explained his ideas about art. His ideas also spread through exhibits of his work in museums around the world. He had a tremendous influence on many artists after his time.

RAMÓN FRADE, *El Pan Nuestro (Our Daily Bread)*.
1905. Oil on canvas. 60¼" x 38¼".
Instituto de Cultura Puertorriqueña, San Juan, Puerto Rico.

Do you think this is a real person?

What is this man carrying?

What do you know about this man?

When Ramón Frade (1875–1954) was born in the town of Cayey, Puerto Rico had been ruled by Spain as a colony for nearly four hundred years. In 1897 Spain granted Puerto Rico the right to govern itself, but seven months later the island was invaded by the United States during the Spanish-American War. The war ended in 1898, and in the peace treaty, Puerto Rico came under American control.

Ramón Frade was a realist, meaning that he tried to paint places, people, and objects as they appear in real life. He created art based on traditional themes, including landscapes and scenes showing the lives of the people of Puerto Rico.

When Frade painted *El Pan Nuestro* in 1905, times were hard in Puerto Rico, especially for poor people. Most of the Spanish companies had left, leaving many unemployed. It was difficult for people to make a living and support their families. American rule had not improved the lives of ordinary people, and many Puerto Ricans longed for independence.

In *El Pan Nuestro* we see an elderly man with bare feet walking toward us. He is standing tall, but his face is lined and weary. This figure is immediately recognizable to any Puerto Rican: he is a *jibaro* (hee-VAH-roe), a farmer who labors on the land. He is shown in earth colors that match the rural landscape around him, making him seem almost one with the earth. He stands out against the brilliant blue sky, and his straw hat surrounds his face like a halo. The long blade of a machete, a knife that is both a tool and a weapon, hangs from his belt. The title of the painting refers to the plantains that the *jibaro* carries in his arms, because this fruit was eaten by most Puerto Ricans every day, often at breakfast, lunch, and dinner.

Frade's painting presents an image of Puerto Rico's national identity, an identity that he and others felt was in danger of disappearing. The man in *El Pan Nuestro* is a symbol for the Puerto Rican struggle to survive; while he may not be wealthy, he is dignified and proud.

JUAN SÁNCHEZ, *Mujer Eterna: Free Spirit Forever (Eternal Woman: Free Spirit Forever)*.
1988. Oil, acrylic, laser prints, collage on canvas. 74½" x 58", diptych.
Collection of the artist.

How many shapes appear more than once in this painting?

How many different images of women can you find?

If you painted someone you love, whom would you choose?

Juan Sánchez (b. 1954) was born in New York City. His parents left Puerto Rico to come to America not long before he was born, and Sánchez considers himself "Nuyorican," a Puerto Rican person who lives in New York. Sánchez remembers starting to draw when he was five years old. He loved drawing cartoon characters from television. His parents encouraged him in his art, and a cousin who worked in a paper factory brought him leftover paper for drawing. When he was in fifth grade, a new art teacher noticed his talent and worked with him after school twice a week. His family could not afford to send him to a Saturday art program at the Pratt Institute, so his teacher raised the money for him to go to art classes.

When he was growing up, Sánchez's parents encouraged him to be proud of his Puerto Rican heritage. In his work, Sánchez combines photographs, drawings, symbols from Taíno and African cultures, fragments of poetry, and collage, with the vibrant colors of the Caribbean. Often his work relates to the idea of memory, either of a person or an event. For Sánchez, creating art from the memories of Puerto Rican people is a way to preserve their history. He feels that when people forget their history, they lose their cultural identity.

Sánchez created *Mujer Eterna: Free Spirit Forever* in remembrance of his mother, Carmen María Colon. In the large center photograph we see her as a beautiful young woman. Surrounding that image are several smaller pictures that show Carmen María at different times in her life. Beneath the photographs are large symbols of Caguana, the Mother Earth figure in Taíno legends. Near the bottom bright flowers and leaves—representing his mother's knowledge of botany (the study of plants)—turn into candy-colored hearts that dance among the photographs. A female goddess figure supports a tombstone-shaped object that contains the large center picture of Carmen María. Sánchez explains, "This painting became a shrine, an altarpiece for my mother's free and ever-inspiring eternal spirit."

Sánchez still works in New York City as a painter, photographer, writer, political activist, and professor of art at Hunter College.

FERNANDO BOTERO, *Joachim Jean Aberbach y Su Familia* (*Joachim Jean Aberbach and His Family*).
1970. Oil on canvas. 92" x 77".
Susan Auerbach Collection, New York.

---  ✧  ---

Describe the shapes that the artist used in this painting.

What are the relationships among the people pictured?

Why did Botero include a house, an animal, and even toys?

Why are all the people so round?

---

Fernando Botero (b. 1932) was born in the town of Medellín, Colombia. The only original art he saw growing up was in churches and chapels, because there were no museums in Medellín. As a teenager he drew illustrations for a large newspaper, and by the age of twenty he had saved enough money to go to Europe. Finally he could see paintings, sculptures, and buildings that he had only seen before in pictures and books.

Botero lived in several European cities while attending art school, and he was strongly influenced by the artworks he found in the great European museums. He spent hours copying the works of master painters such as Diego Velázquez, Leonardo da Vinci, and Peter Paul Rubens. This was Botero's way of learning from many great artists who had lived hundreds of years before him. He explored traditional subjects such as portraiture (pictures of people) and still life (pictures of objects), and he practiced his painting technique.

After four years in Europe, Botero returned to Latin America and developed his own distinct style. He drew from his Colombian heritage and the old masters he had studied in Europe, and he experimented with the illusion of three-dimensional shapes in a flat painting. In his work the subjects look inflated or plumped up. Botero, like some of the old masters, used the suggestion of massive size to emphasize the ideas of solidity and strength.

In *Joachim Jean Aberbach y Su Familia*, Botero created a group portrait of his friend the music publisher Joachim Aberbach and his family. Botero explained, "I started with what was there. The family lived in a house exactly like that." This portrait is different from a typical family photograph with everyone smiling, but their calm expressions recall the faces in many of the European paintings that Botero had studied.

Botero continues to create paintings and sculpture with his distinctive oversize figures and forms. More recently his works have explored themes of violence and power, and his subjects have been the wars in his country and in the Middle East.

DIEGO ISAIAS HERNANDEZ MÉNDEZ, *Peligro de Corte Flores y Bajar Barriletes del Día de los Difuntos*
*(Danger in Picking Flowers and Bringing Down Kites on the Day of the Dead).*
2004. Oil on canvas. 20" x 26".
Collection of Charles Davey. www.artemaya.com.

What are three words you would use to describe this painting?

Why are the children climbing the tree?

What are the colorful circles near the top of the tree?

Are the children in danger?

Diego Isaias Hernandez Méndez (b. 1968) has lived all his life in the Tz'utujil (Zoo-too-HEEL) town of San Juan la Laguna, in the highlands of Guatemala near Lake Atitlán. Tz'utujil is one of twenty-one Maya languages spoken in Guatemala, and the Tz'utujil Maya have lived in the area surrounding Lake Atitlán for hundreds of years.

From the time he was a little boy, Hernández loved to draw. He covered the walls of his room with hundreds of drawings. He is a self-taught artist, meaning that he taught himself how to draw and paint. While the term "folk art" is often used to describe art by self-trained artists, Hernández and other Tz'utujil Maya artists describe their artwork as *pinturas populares*, "paintings of the people." As the Maya of Guatemala enter today's world of computers and television, many of their ancient traditions are in danger of disappearing. The *pinturas populares* document parts of daily life such as cooking tortillas, religious ceremonies, and traditional Maya art forms such as weaving, dancing, and music.

In this painting Hernández depicts a colorful scene from *Día de los Muertos*, the Day of the Dead. In Guatemala and other parts of Latin America, the Day of the Dead is a festival to remember friends and family who have died. Families bring picnic baskets filled with delicious food to the cemetery where their loved ones are buried. In parts of Guatemala it is traditional to create beautiful kites that are flown high into the sky, often with messages tied to their tails for loved ones who have died.

Hernández often shows a moment when an accident has occurred, but rather than create a sad scene, he uses vibrant colors and very active movement. He paints with a sense of humor, but his work makes us think about how people cope with hardships, big and small. The colors and repeated shapes in Hernández's paintings are similar to those found in traditional Maya weavings, which tell the story of a community and are filled with lively colors and complex patterns.

Go back and look through these paintings again.

Which one of the artworks in this book stands out most in your mind today? Why?

What questions would you ask the artist about this work if she or he were here?

If you could go inside one of these artworks, which one would you choose? What would it be like to be inside this work?

What things in these images seem familiar to you? What things seem new?

If you could visit one of the places that you read about in this book, where would you go?

Return to this book another day and you may see things in a different way. You may also discover something new about these Latin American artists.

Keep looking!